Bless Your
HEART!

It's a Kentucky Thing
Y'all Wouldn't Understand

By Michael Crisp

It's a Kentucky Thing: Y'all Wouldn't Understand

by Michael Crisp

Copyright © 2018

1st Edition cover & layout design by Kevin Kifer
www.k2-technology.com

ISBN 978-1-64370-916-1

First Edition

Author Website
www.MICHAELCRISPONLINE.com

Published in Georgetown, KY
Printed in the U.S.A

DEDICATION

This book is dedicated to the teachers of Kentucky. Thanks for your support, encouragement, dedication and inspiration. You make our state a better place.

- Michael Crisp

About This Book

It's no secret – I love words. I make a living as an author, so loving words is practically a job requirement when you do what I do. And while I'm writing, I'm often searching for the perfect words that will help me share a story, convey a feeling or capture a moment.

A few months ago, I was at home having lunch with my wife, Anne, when she showed me a magazine article about the quirky expressions that southerners often use. We had a great time perusing the phrases in the article, as this list of quirky sayings brought back a slew of memories (and quite a few laughs too).

We were already familiar with many of the expressions in the article, like the universally popular "come hell or high water" and "hold your horses", but we were also fascinated with the expressions in the article that were a little more off the beaten path. One of these was "fixin' to", which for me immediately conjured up memories of my good friend Taylor Cannon.

Taylor and my mother, Marge Crisp, worked together as land developers in my hometown of Georgetown during the 1990s. Even though they were business partners, my mother felt incumbent upon herself to consistently make sure Taylor was getting his projects finished in a timely fashion. One might say she thought she needed to "stay on his ass", so to speak. She would usually ask him questions like "did you meet with the inspectors?" or "did you finish the survey?", and he would almost always respond with "I'm fixin' to".

"Yeah, you're always 'fixin' to'," she'd reply sarcastically.

Speaking of my mother, I had heard several of these expressions from her over the years. She probably learned most of these phrases from her childhood in rural Floyd County, and the rest she gleaned from her years as a builder and real estate agent in Scott County. She loved expressions and wasn't afraid to use them, especially the kind of off-color phrases that she had picked up from the many subcontractors that worked for her over the years. In the interest of staying somewhat "family friendly", I'll shy away from these expressions and instead share with you her favorite phrase. It was "I'd like to buy him for what he's worth and sell him for what he thinks he's worth." I love this expression because it's both humorous and profound. It's quintessential Kentucky.

As Anne and I continued reading through the list, there were a few sayings that neither of us had ever heard before, such as "hangin' in there like hair in a biscuit". I don't remember what we had for lunch that day, but thankfully it didn't involve biscuits.

With Anne's encouragement, I decided to write a book about the most popular expressions that we Kentuckians have been known to use. And now you're holding that book in your hands. Ain't that somethin'?!

This book is all about those "perfect words" – words that take us back in time to those simple, fleeting moments in our lives that live forever, thanks in large part to the wonderful words that were shared during those times. Thanks to these fabulous phrases, we are able to reflect fondly on these memories and hold them dear to our hearts. My mom, as well as my friend Taylor are no longer with us – but I would like to think that they would have both enjoyed reading this book just as much as I enjoyed writing it.

Marge Crisp

She would have been happy to "jerk a knot in your tail" if you didn't like this book.

Criteria

Creating this book was fun but also challenging. There were literally hundreds of phrases that I considered including in this list, but ultimately the top 100 expressions that I chose were selected based on the following criteria:

First and foremost, I had to be familiar with the phrases and have had to had heard them at least once in my lifetime. Sure, most of the expressions in this book probably weren't invented in Kentucky, but it was important to me that they have been spoken by a Kentuckian at least a time or two.

Second, I gave preferential treatment to expressions that featured a combination of words rather than just one word. I made a few exceptions to this rule by including a handful of one-word expressions like "Catawampus", "Persnickety" and of course, "Y'all", but the vast majority of phrases in this book feature more than just one word.

Finally, the expressions needed to be timeless and unforgettable. These southern sayings have been around for generations, and it's important that future generations of Kentuckians celebrate them – and better yet use them – in conversations to come. It's up to all of us here in the Bluegrass state to keep these expressions around for a while, and share them with our children before they get to thinking that they're too big for their britches!

#1

"Y'all"

DEFINITION

A shortened way to say "you all" when talking to (or about) 2 or more people.

EXAMPLE

"Y'all better get going or you'll be late!"

FUN FACT

Y'all is the most famous Kentucky expression by far, having been popularized on everything from t-shirts to water towers (thanks Florence, Kentucky)!

Water tower in Florence, Kentucky
courtesy of Wikipedia

#2

"Madder Than a Wet Hen"

DEFINITION

To get very angry.

EXAMPLE

"Grandma's gonna be madder than a wet hen when she finds out you tracked mud all over her floor!"

ORIGIN

When a hen lays its eggs, she usually likes to remain in her nest after her eggs are removed. In order to get the hen to lay more eggs, farmers would typically pull the hen from its nest, dunk her in water, and then place her back in her nest so she could start laying eggs again.

#3

"Bless Your Heart"

DEFINITION

A phrase that usually conveys sympathy or concern, sometimes to help cushion an insult.

EXAMPLE

"Oh, bless your heart - you may not be the smartest girl here tonight but you're definitely the prettiest."

SIMILAR EXPRESSIONS

"Aren't you precious?"
"He/She tries"

#4

"Fixin' To"

DEFINITION

Getting ready to do something.

EXAMPLE

"I'm fixin' to go to town, y'all need anything?"

FUN FACT

"All the fixin's" can be used to describe a big meal that has lots of sides.

#5

"High Falutin'"

DEFINITION

A person who is arrogant or
thinks highly of themselves.

EXAMPLE

"Look at him struttin' in here all high falutin' and such!"

SIMILAR EXPRESSIONS

"Uppity"
"Citified"

A 19th century steamboat

courtesy of Wikipedia

It's not certain how the phrase "high falutin'" came about, but there are 2 theories that have survived the ages. Wealthy travelers in the 19th century would take steamboats, which often had high-fluted funnels on the vessels. It is believed that common folk would sometimes term these steamboat passengers as "high falutin'". Others believe the phrase is derived directly from the musical instrument, the flute itself. Because it's a woodwind, the flute is played with the mouth and therefore held high, near the head, as it's being played. A 'high falutin" person is also sometimes called an "uppity" person.

#6

"Cute as a Button"

A way to compliment a child's appearance.

*"Well aren't you precious in your little outfit?
Aren't you just cute as a button?!"*

The oldest button that has ever been found was
discovered in modern-day Pakistan and is believed to
be over 5,000 years old.

#7

"All Gussied Up"

DEFINITION

Dressed in a very formal or fancy manner.

EXAMPLE

We're just going to Wal-Mart, so no sense in getting all gussied up!

FUN FACT

This phrase originates from the term 'gussy', which was popular slang in the 1940s for someone who was overly dressed.

#8

"Two Peas in a Pod"

Two people who are very similar, so much so that they are almost indistinguishable.

"You'd think Jenny and Sarah were twin sisters rather than just friends. With the way they look and act like each other, they're just like two peas in a pod!"

Popular types of peas include the Sugarsnap, Meteor, and Oregon Sugar Pod.

#9

"What in Tarnation?"

DEFINITION

What in the hell?

EXAMPLE

"What in tarnation are you doing to that poor animal?!"

SIMILAR EXPRESSIONS

"What the heck?"
"what in blue blazes?"
"heavens to Betsy"

#10

"Drunker than Cooter Brown"

DEFINITION

The state of being heavily intoxicated.

EXAMPLE

"You keep drinkin' that moonshine and you'll end up drunker than Cooter Brown!"

SIMILAR EXPRESSIONS

"Drunker than a monkey"
"drunk as a skunk"
"dog drunk"

Cooter Brown

courtesy of Wikipedia

It's not known if Cooter Brown (or 'Cootie' Brown,as he is sometimes called) actually existed, but that doesn't stop people from invoking his name to this day as part of this classic phrase. Legend has it that Cooter Brown was a southern man that lived very close to the Mason-Dixon Line during the 1860s, and in order to avoid being drafted by either the armies of the North and the South, stayed perpetually drunk (which made him ineligible for military service during the Civil War). Go figure.

#11

"Pitch a Hissy Fit"

DEFINITION

To throw a tantrum.

EXAMPLE

"You're gonna eat everything on your plate. No need to pitch a hissy fit about it."

SIMILAR EXPRESSIONS

"Have a conniption"
"have a conniption fit"

14

#12

"Over Yonder"

Over there.

"Just head over yonder and you'll run right into it."

"Yonder" is an actual word of Germanic, Dutch and English origin, meaning "at some distance in the direction indicated".

#13

"Good Lord Willing and the Creek Don't Rise"

DEFINITION

A way to express cautious optimism.

EXAMPLE

"I just put air in the tires, and that should get us to Corbin safe and sound, if God willing and the creek don't rise."

FUN FACT

Kentucky has over 90,000 miles of streams within the state.

A Peaceful Creek

courtesy of Wikipedia

The origin of this popular phrase is frequently debated. The expression appeared in magazines and newspapers throughout the 1800s, and the general interpretation was that the "creek" (sometimes "crick") referred to a body of water. As the years passed, another theory about the expression was borne. Legend had it that the expression had actually been coined by Benjamin Hawkins, a political figure from Georgia in the late 18th century and early 19th century. Hawkins worked closely with Native American tribes, specifically the Creek, and eventually married a Creek woman. It was said that in a letter to the president of the United States, Hawkins wrote that he would return to Washington "if God willing and the Creek don't rise", and that by capitalizing "Creek" he was referring to the Indian tribe. To date, no evidence of this letter has ever been found, likely meaning that it is just an urban legend. In any case, the origin of this phrase is destined to remain a mystery.

#14

"Slicker Than Snot (on a Door Knob)"

DEFINITION

Very slippery.

EXAMPLE

"I haven't shoveled the snow off the driveway yet, so be careful - it's slicker than snot on a door knob!"

FUN FACT

A sneeze can travel up to 100 miles per hour.

#15

"Hangin' in There Like Hair in a Biscuit"

DEFINITION

Being tenacious.

EXAMPLE

"Our team is playing tough today – we're hangin' in there like hair in a biscuit!"

FUN FACT

There are 185 calories in a biscuit from KFC.

#16

"I'd Rather Be Nibbled to Death by Ducks Than…"

DEFINITION

A way to describe something annoying.

EXAMPLE

"I'd rather be nibbled to death by ducks than to hear your Grandpa tell that story again."

FUN FACT

Male ducks are called drakes, female ducks are called hens, and baby ducks are called ducklings.

#17

"Old Codge"

An elderly man, often eccentric or curmudgeonly.

"He's still alive? I thought that old codge died years ago!"

"Codge" is derived from the English word "cadge", which was commonly used in the sport of falconry. The "cadge" (or "cage") that housed the falcons would typically be carried by elderly men, who served as assistants (much like "caddies" in golf) to the younger falconers. Over the years, beggars and tramps would often be referred to as "cadges" or "cadgers".

#18

"A Coon's Age"

DEFINITION

A really long time.

EXAMPLE

"How's Becky been doing? Lord, I haven't seen her in a coon's age."

FUN FACT

The average life span of a raccoon is 13 years.

#19

"Jerk a Knot in Your Tail"

DEFINITION

Give someone a spanking.

EXAMPLE

"If you don't listen to me I'll jerk a knot in your tail so fast it'll make your head spin!"

SIMILAR EXPRESSIONS

"I'll bust your tail"
"I'll whup your hind end"
"I'll cream your corn"

#20

"Fair to Middlin'"

Describing something that is
average, or moderately good.

*"How am I doing? Fair to middlin', I suppose. I can't
complain."*

'Middling' is a Scottish word that means 'of medium or
moderate size, strength and quality', and by the 19th
century, the phrase 'fair to middling' was being used
by authors such as Mark Twain and Louisa May Alcott
in some of their most famous works. It also became
a popular phrase in the cotton business, as 'fair to
middling' was often used to describe the grades of
cotton available for purchase.

These sheep look like they're feeling fair to middlin'.
courtesy of Wikipedia

#21

"Look Like Death Eatin' a Cracker"

DEFINITION

An awful or gaunt appearance.

EXAMPLE

"You've lost way too much weight, Darlene. You look just like death eatin' a cracker!"

SIMILAR EXPRESSIONS

"Look like you've been chewed up and spit out"
"spread out like a cold supper"
"look like 10 miles of bad road"

#22

"Don't Have Enough Sense to Pour Piss Out of a Boot"

DEFINITION

A person who isn't very smart.

EXAMPLE

"Billy ain't very bright, that's for sure. He don't have enough sense to pour piss out of a boot if the instructions were written on the heel."

SIMILAR EXPRESSIONS

"If he had an idea, it would die of loneliness"
"he's only got one oar in the water"
"the porch light's on but nobody's home"

#23

"Keep Your Britches On"

DEFINITION

Settle down and compose yourself.

EXAMPLE

"There's no need to rush. Just keep your britches on and you'll get there soon enough."

ORIGIN

This phrase is derived from "keep your shirt on", which was a popular expression in the 19th century. Because clothing was somewhat tight and restrictive during this time, brawls would often begin with angry men taking their shirts off to improve their arms' mobility during a fight.

#24

"Ain't Seen Hide nor Hair"

DEFINITION

Unable to find someone or something.

EXAMPLE

"Will you go find your brother for me? I ain't seed hide nor hair of him all day!"

ORIGIN

This phrase dates back to the 18th century, when hunting and tracking skills were often needed to feed yourself and your family. After shooting your prey, it would sometime escape into the woods or underbrush to elude capture. In many instances, injured prey would soon die but not be found until many days later when their hides or hair where discovered by other hunters.

#25

"Persnickety"

DEFINITION

Finicky or particular.

EXAMPLE

"Quit being so damn persnickety and eat your mashed potatoes!"

ORIGIN

This Scottish word, which dates back to the 19th century, is derived from the word "pernickety", which means "fastidious."

#26

"Busier Than a One-Armed Paper Hanger"

DEFINITION

Very busy.

EXAMPLE

"I wish I could help you right now, but I just don't have the time. I'm busier than a one-armed paper hanger!"

SIMILAR EXPRESSIONS

"Busier than a one-legged cat in a sandbox"
"busier than a moth in a mitten"
"busy as a bee"

#27

"I Reckon"

DEFINITION

I think so.

EXAMPLE

"I haven't seen the casserole dish, but I reckon it's around here somewhere."

ORIGIN

"Reckon" is actually an old English word meaning "to recount or relate". Similar words in other languages include "rekenen" (Dutch) and "rechnen" (German).

#28

"Catawampus"

DEFINITION

Crooked, misshapen or appearing askew.

EXAMPLE

"Straighten up that picture frame; it looks all catawampus hanging on that wall."

ORIGIN

This unique word is likely derived from the words "cater", which means "to move diagonally", and "wampish", a Scottish word that means "to wriggle, swift or turn about".

#29

"Finer Than Frog Hair (Split 3 Ways)"

DEFINITION

Someone (or something) that is attractive.

EXAMPLE

"That girl is finer than frog hair split 3 ways!"

FUN FACT

Although they generally do not have hair, an African species of frog called the Hairy Frog has ridges of small black spines on the back of their bodies that look very much like hair.

#30

"About as Useless as Teats on a Boar Hog"

DEFINITION

A way to describe a lazy person.

EXAMPLE

"Aw, don't mind him none, he's about as useless as teats on a boar hog."

SIMILAR EXPRESSIONS

"He won't hit a lick at a snake"
"About as useless as a steering wheel on a mule"

#31

"As the Crow Flies"

DEFINITION

Not too far from here.

EXAMPLE

"It's about a mile away as the crow flies. You'll get there in no time."

FUN FACT

A group of crows is called a murder.

#32

"Handier Than a Pocket on a Shirt"

DEFINITION

Very useful.

EXAMPLE

"My new Swiss Army knife can do just about anything. It's handier than a pocket on a shirt."

ORIGIN

The word pocket is derived from the French word "poque", which means "bag".

courtesy of Wikipedia

#33

"Filthy as Cairn"

DEFINITION

Dirty or grimy.

EXAMPLE

"Go wash your face before dinner, son, it's filthy as cairn!"

SIMILAR EXPRESSIONS

"Look like you were raised in a barn"
"look like a pig sty"

#34

"Grinnin' Like a Possum Eating Briers"

DEFINITION

Appearing both happy and mischievous.

EXAMPLE

"Becky was up all night studying for that test, and she just knows she's gonna pass it with flying colors. She's grinnin' like a possum eating briars!"

FUN FACT

The town of Possum Trot, Kentucky, is located in Marshall County between Paducah and Calvert City.

#35

"Are Your Arms (or Legs) Broke?"

DEFINITION

Why can't you do it yourself?

EXAMPLE

"Get you a pop? You're standing right next to the refrigerator, why don't you get it? Are your arms broke?"

FUN FACT

There are 4 bones found in the human leg: the femur, the patella, the tibia, and the fibula.

#36

"Don't Have a Pot to Piss in"

DEFINITION

Very poor.

EXAMPLE

"We grew up poor, that's for sure. We didn't have a pot to piss in or a window to throw it out of."

SIMILAR EXPRESSIONS

"Too poor to paint, too proud to whitewash"
"so broke I can't pay attention"
"as poor as a church mouse"

#37

"Pig in a Poke"

A surprise revealed at the end of a trick or a scam.

"I can't believe I voted for that guy. All of his promises turned out to be pigs in a poke!"

This phrase originated many years ago in the farmers' markets of old England. Pigs were a popular item at these markets, and merchants selling pigs would often carry them in "pokes", which are sacks or bags. Unscrupulous merchants were known to replace the pig with an animal of lesser value, such as a cat, and keep it hidden in the poke until the transaction was complete. The merchant would then abscond with the money and the buyer would have been duped into purchasing an item that they didn't want to buy. This scenario is also where we get the phrase "letting the cat out of the bag".

#38

"I'd Like to Buy Him for What He's Worth and Sell Him for What He Thinks He's Worth"

DEFINITION

Describing someone who is prideful.

EXAMPLE

"Phillip is so full of himself that I'd like to buy him for what he's worth and sell him for what he thinks he's worth!"

SIMILAR EXPRESSIONS

"He's stuck up higher than a light pole"
"he's so stuck up, he'd drown in a rainstorm"
"he thinks the sun comes up just to hear him crow"

#39

"A Hot Mess"

DEFINITION

Someone who is disorganized or very busy.

EXAMPLE

"I'm sorry, I must look like a hot mess right now!"

FUN FACT

A "mess" can also describe a large helping of something, like a "mess of collard greens".

#40

"Older Than Dirt (or Methuselah)"

DEFINITION

Someone who is very elderly or ancient.

EXAMPLE

"You mean to tell me that Lisa's grandpa is still alive? He's gotta be older than dirt!"

SIMILAR EXPRESSIONS

"Older than the hills"
"older than God"

#41

"Scarce as Hen's Teeth"

DEFINITION

Very rare or hard to find.

EXAMPLE

"I've looked high and low but I can't find anywhere that I can buy a good bourbon barrel. They're about as scarce as hen's teeth."

FUN FACT

Hens don't actually have teeth.

#42

"I'll Snatch You Bald-Headed"

DEFINITION

I'll pull out all of your hair.

EXAMPLE

"Don't let me catch you sneaking out again tonight or I'll wring your neck and snatch you bald-headed!"

SIMILAR EXPRESSIONS

"I'm gonna cut your tail"
"Me 'n you is gonna mix"
"I'll slap you to sleep and then slap you for sleeping"

#43

"Rode Hard and Put Up Wet"

DEFINITION

To appear unkempt or look exhausted.

EXAMPLE

"Lord, that girl looks like she's been rode hard and put up wet."

ORIGIN

While a horse is being ridden or exercised, it can sweat quite a bit. It's generally best to walk it around before being put back in the stable, so the horse can dry off and not appear so rough.

courtesy of Wikipedia

#44

"A Fer Piece"

DEFINITION

Far away.

EXAMPLE

"We lived a fer piece down the road when I was a kid, so much so that we had to pipe in the sunshine."

FUN FACT

Kentucky's highest point, Black Mountain, has an elevation of 4,145 feet. That sure is a fer piece!

#45

"He Could Eat Corn Through a Picket Fence"

DEFINITION

A way to describe a person with bucked teeth.

EXAMPLE

"That poor kid needs braces in the worst way. He could eat corn through a picket fence."

FUN FACT

Most picket fences in the United States range between 36" or 48" in height.

#46

"Colder Than a Well-Digger's Ass"

Very chilly.

"Turn the damn thermostat up, will you? It's colder than a well-digger's ass in here!"

"Colder than a witch's tit"
"colder than a polar bear's toenails"

#47

"I'm Gonna Learn You"

DEFINITION

I'm going to teach you.

EXAMPLE

"I'm gonna learn you right good!"

FUN FACT

You're learning lots of new things about Kentucky phrases just by reading this book!

#48

"Pert Near But Not Plumb"

DEFINITION

Pretty good but not perfect.

EXAMPLE

"That picture hanging on the wall is pert near but not plumb. Move it just a bit to the left and that'll center it."

SIMILAR EXPRESSIONS

"Close but no cigar"

#49

"Believe You Me"

DEFINITION

Believe me.

EXAMPLE

"Believe you me, I'll wear you out if you don't mow that grass."

ORIGIN

Adding an extra word for emphasis in a sentence, whether it's grammatically correct or not, can be found many times in older written works, including Shakespeare ("And bid her, mark you me, on Wednesday next" from Romeo and Juliet) and the Bible ("They need not depart; give them ye to eat" from the Book of Matthew 14:16, King James version).

#50

"My Ears are Burning"

Someone is gossiping about me right now.

"You told the girls I flunked that test? Oh, my ears are burning right now with what they're saying about me."

This phrase harkens back to Roman times. Philosophers such as Pliny and Plautus believed that if your right ear was burning you were being praised, but if your left ear was burning you were "the subject of evil intent."

#51

"Shittin' in Tall Cotton"

Living well and doing great.

"Once we win the Powerball jackpot, we'll be shittin' in tall cotton for sure!"

A field of cotton that was "tall" was considered a healthy crop, and deemed more valuable than a cotton field that had an average height. This phrase likely began as "sittin' in tall cotton" but morphed over the years into its present form.

#52

"Don't Have the Sense God Gave a Goose"

Not very smart or intelligent.

"Oh, Dave doesn't know what he's talking about. He don't have the sense God gave a goose."

According to *Game and Fish* magazine, most migrating geese find their way into western Kentucky via the Mississippi Flyway.

#53

"Sexy as Socks on a Rooster"

DEFINITION

Very unattractive.

EXAMPLE

"Warsh that makeup off, it makes you look about as sexy as socks on a rooster."

SIMILAR EXPRESSIONS

"Ugly as homemade sin"
"he's got a face that would stop an 8-day clock"
"fell out of the ugly tree and hit every branch on the way down"

#54

"It's So Dry the Trees Are Bribin' the Dogs"

A drought or long period of time without rain.

"Somebody done pissed off God 'cause it ain't rained for two weeks. It's so dry the trees are bribin' the dogs!"

Kentucky's average annual rainfall is between 40-50 inches, with approximately half of this rain coming between April and September.

#55

"Well That Just Dills My Pickle"

DEFINITION

That makes me upset.

EXAMPLE

"She cut in front of you at the grocery store? Well that just dills my pickle!"

SIMILAR EXPRESSIONS

"Well that just gets my goat"
"well that just burns my ass"

#56

"Dreckly"

Something that you'll do eventually
but not immediately.

"I'll be there dreckly."

"Right quick"

#57

"They Got More ____ than Carter's Got Liver Pills"

DEFINITION

Having an abundance of, or having
much more than one needs.

EXAMPLE

*"That family's always been rich. They got more money
than Carter's got liver pills!"*

ORIGIN

In the first half of the 20th century, Carter's Little Liver Pills could
be found in many family's medicine cabinets throughout the United
States. Advertisements for these pills claimed that they would cure
a wide variety of ailments and increase bile flow in the liver. They
were so plentiful in fact that the phrase "he/she's got more ____
than Carter's got liver pills" became commonplace. Ironically, the
Federal Trade Commission required the medicine to remove "Liver"
from its name in 1951 after it was proven that the pills had no effect
- good or otherwise - on a person's liver.

Now that's a lot of pills.

courtesy of Wikipedia

#58

"Fuller Than a Tick on a Coon Hound's Back"

DEFINITION

Overstuffed, filled up and nearly bursting.

EXAMPLE

"Thank you, but I can't eat one more bite. I'm fuller than a tick on a coon hound's back."

SIMILAR EXPRESSIONS

"Stuffed to the gills"

#59

"Knee-High to a Grasshopper"

DEFINITION

Very short or very small.

EXAMPLE

"My have you've grown up! I haven't seen you since you were knee-high to a grasshopper!"

ORIGIN

The phrase began in the early 1800s as "knee-high to a frog", and sometimes other animals like jackrabbits, bumblebees and mosquitoes would be used along the way, but "grasshopper" tends to be the most popular variation of the saying.

#60

"Dad Gum It"

DEFINITION

A Kentucky "cuss" word that expresses annoyance.

EXAMPLE

"Dad gum it, if you change the radio station again I'll wring your neck!"

SIMILAR EXPRESSIONS

"Jeez o' Pete"
"dammit to hell"
"dad blast it"
"dad burn it"
"doggone it"

#61

"I'd Give My Eye Teeth for That"

To want something very badly.

"Of course I'd love to go out with her - she's the prettiest girl in school. You know I'd give my eye teeth for that."

Your eye teeth are actually called canines. They are called "eye teeth" because they usually lie directly beneath your eyes.

#62

"Ran Like a Scalded Haint"

Fled because of fear or fright.

"When he saw that guy coming at him with a baseball bat, Derek ran like a scalded haint."

A "haint" is a southern word for "ghost", and it's believed that scalding one with fire or hot water will quickly vanquish the spirit.

#63

"Drier Than a Popcorn Fart"

DEFINITION

Very dry.

EXAMPLE

"It'd be nice if a cool breeze came through here, because it's drier than a popcorn fart."

FUN FACT

Kentucky is one of the top 9 popcorn producing states in the country (the others are Iowa, Indiana, Illinois, Kansas, Michigan, Missouri, Nebraska and Ohio).

#64

"Dead as a Door Nail"

Dead or appearing lifeless.

"They put that murderer in the electric chair this morning, so right now he's probably dead as a doornail."

The phrase comes from the 14th century poem *The Vision of William Concerning Piers Plowman*, written by William Langland.

#65

"Going to Hell in a Handbasket"

#66

"Young'ns"

DEFINITION

Children or young people.

EXAMPLE

"You young'ns better finish your homework if you know what's good for you."

SIMILAR EXPRESSIONS

"Rugrats"
"whippersnappers"

#67

"All Tucker'd Out"

DEFINITION

Extremely tired.

EXAMPLE

"I'm tired because I'm all tucker'd out from working all day!"

ORIGIN

"Tucker" is a 19th century word that originated in New England, and is defined as "to be weary". It comes from the English word "tuck", which means "to punish or torment".

#68

"He Don't Know Shit from Shinola"

This product probably worked much better than the alternative option.

courtesy of Wikipedia

#69

"Nervous as a Long-Tailed Cat in a Roomful of Rocking Chairs"

DEFINITION

Acting very skittish and fidgety.

EXAMPLE

"Don't worry about the test results, everything's gonna be fine. No need to act as nervous as a long-tailed cat in a roomful of rocking chairs."

FUN FACT

Benjamin Franklin once designed a rocking chair that included a foot pedal that activated an overhead fan.

#70

"He Wouldn't Give a Nickel to See Jesus Ridin' a Bicycle"

DEFINITION

Someone who is miserly and thrifty.

EXAMPLE

"He's so cheap, he wouldn't give a nickel to see Jesus ridin' a bicycle!"

SIMILAR EXPRESSIONS

"He's tighter than the bark on a tree"
"he squeezes a quarter so tight the eagle screams"

#71

"Running Around Like a Chicken With Its Head Cut Off"

Acting manic and unorganized.

"I know you're excited, but you need to calm down for a minute. You're running around like a chicken with its head cut off!"

Although Colonel Harland Sanders began selling his famous fried chicken at the restaurant he owned in Corbin, Kentucky, the first official Kentucky Fried Chicken restaurant opened in Salt Lake City, Utah in 1952.

#72

"Slower than Molasses"

Moving very slow.

"Hurry up and get moving, boy, you're slower than molasses running uphill in winter!"

"Slower than a month of Sundays"
"slow as the day is long"

#73

"Well Butter My Butt and Call Me a Biscuit"

DEFINITION

An expression of shock and surprise.

EXAMPLE

"Jeff took Arlene to the dance? Well butter my butt and call me a biscuit!"

SIMILAR EXPRESSIONS

"Shut my mouth"
"well paint me green and call me a cucumber"
"well pin my tail and call me a donkey"

#74

"Dumber Than Rocks"

DEFINITION

Very stupid.

EXAMPLE

"He might be dumber than rocks, but he's the best looking boy in class."

FUN FACT

Agate is Kentucky's official state rock, although by geological definition it is actually a variety of mineral quartz rather than a rock.

#75

"Hem 'n Haw"

DEFINITION

To stall or procrastinate.

EXAMPLE

"There's no need to hem 'n haw over it, just go do it!"

ORIGIN

This phrase, which dates back to the 15th century, originates from the sounds that someone makes while clearing their throat. These noises, sometimes called "hem and hawk" or "hum and ha", are often made by a person who is stalling for time or searching for a response.

#76

"Untellin'"

Unknown or unimaginable.

"Michael says he's from Georgetown, but it's untellin' where he's really from."

Based in Frankfort, the Kentucky Storytelling Association is a non-profit group that promotes the art, history and performance of storytelling throughout the state.

#77

"Take a Swig"

DEFINITION

To take a drink.

EXAMPLE

"Take a swig of that moonshine and tell me if you think it tastes good."

SIMILAR EXPRESSIONS

"Take a chug"
"turn it up and kill it"

#78

"Six One Way, Half Dozen the Other"

A way to describe two different actions in which the results would be the same.

"We can take the bypass, but it's just as fast to go through town. It's six one way, half dozen the other."

In Kentucky, there is a strange law that makes it illegal to sell a rabbit with dyed fur unless you are selling 6 or more at the same time. The law also applies to baby chicks and ducklings with dyed feathers as well.

#79

"That Dog Don't Hunt Here"

DEFINITION

An unacceptable idea or excuse.

EXAMPLE

"The judge didn't believe my story. He told me 'that dog don't hunt here' before ordering me to pay that fine."

FUN FACT

According to Time magazine, the 3 most popular breeds of dogs in Kentucky are beagles, German shepherds and Labrador retrievers.

**This dog is probably hunting for
a good place to take a nap.**

courtesy of Wikipedia

#80

"You're Gonna Have to Relick that Calf"

DEFINITION

You need to repeat a task that you just did.

EXAMPLE

"I know that you just washed the windows, but I can still see dirt on them. You're gonna have to relick that calf."

SIMILAR EXPRESSIONS

"You're gonna have to chew that cabbage twice."

#81

"Don't Pay Them No Mind"

DEFINITION

Don't listen to them.

EXAMPLE

"Don't pay them no mind, Martha. Those girls are just giggling because they're jealous of you, that's all."

ORIGIN

This expression is a variant of the phrase "pay no heed".

#82

"Happy as a Dead Pig in the Sunshine"

When a pig dies outdoors, its skin usually shrivels up fairly quickly in the warm sun. This is especially true with the skin around its jaw line, as the shriveling around its mouth can give the impression that the dead pig is smiling.

#83

"Nuttier than a Fruitcake"

DEFINITION

Crazy or idiotic.

EXAMPLE

"Don't listen to Mabel, she's nuttier than a fruitcake."

SIMILAR EXPRESSIONS

"Squirrelly"
"crazy as hell"

#84

"Spittin' Image"

An exact duplicate.

"Well look at you, Loretta. You are the spittin' image of your mother."

A 19th century English phrase that is short for "the spit and image of", this expression is used when comparing two people or things that look exactly alike. It's formed from the notion that a person could so closely resemble another that they might be formed by the spit of another.

Famous Kentucky musical duo the Everly Brothers

courtesy of Wikipedia

#85

"Fiddlesticks"

The word "fiddlesticks" was first used in a nonsensical manner in 1600 when it appeared in a line of the Thomas Nashe play Summer's Last Will and Testament.

#86

"Higher than a Cat's Back"

Intoxicated or under the influence of a drug

I don't know what Billy's been smokin',
'cause he's actin' higher than a cat's back!'

A mountain lion was spotted in Bourbon County in December 2014, marking the first time in over 20 years that a mountain lion had been sighted in Kentucky.

#87

"Lower Than a Snake's Belly in a Wagon Rut"

DEFINITION

A way to describe someone with no morals.

EXAMPLE

"Almost every politician I've ever met has been lower than a snake's belly in a wagon rut."

FUN FACT

Garrard County, Kentucky, was a small stop along a wagon trail that spanned between the east coast of the United States and Texas in the 1880s.

#88

"I'll Be On You Like White on Rice"

DEFINITION

I'm going to be watching you closely.

EXAMPLE

"You better watch out, 'cause I'm gonna be on you like white on rice!"

ORIGIN

The phrase first appeared in print in 1951 book *Iron City* by author Lloyd L. Brown.

#89

"Naked as a Jaybird"

DEFINITION

Nude or wearing very little clothing.

EXAMPLE

"Put a damn diaper on that baby, it's naked as a jaybird!"

SIMILAR EXPRESSIONS

"Buck naked"
"butt naked"

#90

"Piddle"

DEFINITION

To waste time.

EXAMPLE

"I haven't been doing much today, and I'll probably just piddle later on tonight."

ORIGIN

This British word, meaning "to spend time in a wasteful or ineffective way", first began appearing in the print in the mid 16th century. In Great Britain, the word is also slang for "to urinate".

#91

"I'll Tan Your Hide"

I'll spank you.

"Talk back to me again and I'll tan your hide!"

In reality, the process of tanning a hide is done by soaking it in a chemical liquid or by exposing it to ultraviolet rays (typically the sun). No spanking or beating required!

#92

"Short End of the Stick"

Receiving the worst outcome in a situation.

"You mean to tell me that everyone else got catfish to eat and I'm just gonna get hush puppies? I should've know I'd get the short end of the stick."

This expression began in the 16th century as "short end of the staff", but developed into "short end of the stick" over time. There are various theories behind the phrase's actual meaning, but many folks believe it's a reference to the game of drawing straws (or sticks) to see who has to do an unpleasant task.

#93

"Barking Up the Wrong Tree"

DEFINITION

Making a wrong assumption.

EXAMPLE

"Roger thinks that is ex-wife took all that money, but I think he's barking up the wrong tree."

ORIGIN

This American expression comes from the early 19th century, when packs of dogs were used for hunting. Often the animals being hunted would scurry noisily into a group of trees in order to confuse the pursuing dogs, which would sometimes confuse the canines into mistakenly believing the prey were trapped atop a tree when in fact they had escaped.

#94

"Gimme Some Sugar"

DEFINITION

Kiss me.

EXAMPLE

"Won't you come over here and gimme some sugar?"

SIMILAR EXPRESSIONS

"Gimme a smooch"
"lay one on me"

#95

"I'm Beside Myself"

I'm worried or distraught.

"I'm just beside myself worrying if I left the stove on or not."

Andrew Harrison played alongside his twin brother, Aaron, on the University of Kentucky's 2013-14 and 2014-15 basketball teams.

#96

"Stompin' Grounds"

DEFINITION

The place where you grew up
or spent your formative years.

EXAMPLE

"You're from Sadieville? Well that's my old stompin' grounds!"

ORIGIN

Originally called "stamping grounds", this 19th century American phrase refers to a field or farm where cattle are usually gathered.

#97

"Quit Being Ugly"

Stop acting angry or disrespectful.

"There's no need to fight over that last piece of pizza. Quit being ugly with each other and figure out how you're gonna share it."

There is actually a band called Kentucky Ugly. They are a 3-piece "southern metal" group from the Danville, Kentucky area.

#98

"Citified"

A way to describe someone from the country who has been "softened" by living in the city.

"Billy's been actin' all citified since he moved into town."

Kentucky's four largest cities (by population) are Louisville, Lexington, Bowling Green and Owensboro.

#99

"Hold Your Horses"

DEFINITION

Slow down and think before
making an important decision.

EXAMPLE

*"Hold your horses, son, we'll get there when we get
there."*

FUN FACT

Aristides won the very first Kentucky Derby, which took
place in 1875.

#100

"Be Careful"

DEFINITION

Goodbye.

EXAMPLE

"Okay, sounds good, be careful."

SIMILAR EXPRESSIONS

"Have a Goodin"

Feel free to add

any of your other

favorite Kentucky

expressions:

add to the list

- [ ] 101. _____
- [ ] 102. _____
- [ ] 103. _____
- [ ] 104. _____
- [ ] 105. _____
- [ ] 106. _____
- [ ] 107. _____
- [ ] 108. _____
- [ ] 109. _____
- [ ] 110. _____
- [ ] 111. _____
- [ ] 112. _____
- [ ] 113. _____
- [ ] 114. _____
- [ ] 115. _____

add to the list

☐ 116. _____

☐ 117. _____

☐ 118. _____

☐ 119. _____

☐ 120. _____

☐ 121. _____

☐ 122. _____

☐ 123. _____

☐ 124. _____

☐ 125. _____

☐ 126. _____

☐ 127. _____

☐ 128. _____

☐ 129. _____

☐ 130. _____

add to the list

☐ 131. _____

☐ 132. _____

☐ 133. _____

☐ 134. _____

☐ 135. _____

☐ 136. _____

☐ 137. _____

☐ 138. _____

☐ 139. _____

☐ 140. _____

☐ 141. _____

☐ 142. _____

☐ 143. _____

☐ 144. _____

☐ 145. _____

add to the list

- ☐ 146. _____
- ☐ 147. _____
- ☐ 148. _____
- ☐ 149. _____
- ☐ 150. _____
- ☐ 151. _____
- ☐ 152. _____
- ☐ 153. _____
- ☐ 154. _____
- ☐ 155. _____
- ☐ 156. _____
- ☐ 157. _____
- ☐ 158. _____
- ☐ 159. _____
- ☐ 160. _____

add to the list

☐ 161. _____

☐ 162. _____

☐ 163. _____

☐ 164. _____

☐ 165. _____

☐ 166. _____

☐ 167. _____

☐ 168. _____

☐ 169. _____

☐ 170. _____

☐ 171. _____

☐ 172. _____

☐ 173. _____

☐ 174. _____

☐ 175. _____

References

It was a lot of work in researching and writing this book, so I'd like to thank some of my most valuable resources that were helpful to me along the way:

Kentucky Tourism

Wander Wisdom

The Lexington Herald Leader

Wikipedia

OnlyInYourState.com

50States.com

Movoto.com

Southern Living

The Huffington Post

Sheknows.com

Dictionary.com

Country Living

Special Thanks

Conner Crisp

Herman Crisp

Anne Huber

Ella Huber

Holly Huber

Daniel Huber

Tasha Huber

David Sloan

John McDaniel

John Sutton

Stacey Gillespie

Kevin Kifer

Han Fan

Andrew Moore

Scott McBrayer

Kenny Rice

Scott Hall

Roger Michael

Nathan Benge

Kelly Jo Stull

David Goldman

Brandon Green

Marge Crisp

It's a Kentucky Thing: Y'all Wouldn't Understand
written by
Michael Crisp

MICHAEL'S BOOKS INCLUDE:

The Best Kentucky Trivia Book Ever

The Kentucky Bucket List: 100 Ways to
Have a Real Kentucky Experience

The Kentucky Bucket List - Part 2: 100 More Ways
to Have a Real Kentucky Experience

The Tennessee Bucket List: 100 Ways to
Have a Real Tennessee Experience

The Ohio Bucket List: 100 Ways to
Have a Real Ohio Experience

Murder in the Mountains:
The Muriel Baldridge Story

The Making of The Very Worst Thing

Blue Shirts

MICHAEL'S FILMS INCLUDE:

The Very Worst Thing

When Happy Met Froggie

Legendary: When Baseball
Came to the Bluegrass

A Cut Above: The Legend of Larry Roberts

A Life of Its Own

The Death of Floyd Collins

Taken Too Soon: The Katelyn Markham Story

MICHAELCRISPONLINE.COM

"Simplicity is the glory of expression."
- Walt Whitman